potatoes

potatoes

Annie Nichols

Photography by Peter Myers

RYLAND
PETERS
& SMALL

LONDON NEW YORK

Designer *Fiona Tweedie*
Commissioning Editor *Elsa Petersen-Schepelern*
Editor *Sharon Ashman*
Production *Patricia Harrington*
Art Director *Gabriella Le Grazie*
Publishing Director *Alison Starling*

Food Stylist *Annie Nichols*
Stylist *Wei Tang*

First published in the United States in 2003
by Ryland Peters & Small, Inc.
519 Broadway, 5th Floor
New York, NY 10012
www.rylandpeters.com

10 9 8 7 6 5 4 3 2 1

Library of Congress Cataloging-in-Publication Data

Nichols, Annie.
  Potatoes / Annie Nichols ; photography by Peter Myers.
    p. cm.
Includes index.
  ISBN 1-84172-490-4
  1. Cookery (Potatoes) 2. Cookery, International. I. Title.
TX803.P3N53 2003
641.6'521--dc21
                              2003005928

NOTES

All potatoes and other vegetables are washed then
peeled in the usual way, unless otherwise noted.
Where relevant, a particular type of potato is specified in
the recipes, such as baking or salad. Where the type of
potato is not specified, use either variety.
Ovens should be preheated to the specified temperature.
If using a convection oven, cooking times should be
reduced according to manufacturer's instructions.

Recipes in this book have previously been published in
Potatoes: from Mash to Fries by Annie Nichols.

contents

DEDICATION

To Winnie and Fred Nichols, my
Mum and Dad, for a childhood full
of wholesome food, especially Dad's
new potatoes—the best in the west.

the basics

BOILING AND STEAMING POTATOES

 New potatoes should be cooked in boiling salted water—old potatoes put in a saucepan of cold salted water then brought to a boil. Don't test for tenderness until towards the end of cooking time, or the potatoes will absorb water, become soggy, and fall apart. Most of the nutrients are found just under the skin of the potato, so leave the skin on when boiling, and peel only after cooking. Peeled potatoes also absorb more water while they are cooking. Steaming takes a little longer than boiling. Boil or steam similar-size potatoes together to make sure they cook evenly.

MASHING POTATOES

 Soft, fluffy, and creamy—mashed potato is the epitome of comfort food. It can be served as a side dish, as a dish in its own right, or used as the basis for many other recipes, such as croquettes or potato cakes. Potatoes cooked in their skins retain nutrients and have a dry texture that absorbs liquids and flavorings better. If boiling peeled chunks of potato, drain when cooked, return to the saucepan, and let steam dry for a few minutes. Mash with a potato masher or fork for a coarse texture, or press through a potato ricer or food mill, or push through a sieve for a fluffy, light texture. For an even lighter texture, heat liquids such as milk or cream, then beat into the mashed potato.

Classic mashed potato recipe

Scrub 2½ lb. medium potatoes, such as russet or long white. Boil in lightly salted water for 20–30 minutes, or until tender. Drain, cool, and peel, then mash in a stick of butter. Reheat, season, then beat in 1½ cups hot milk.

ROASTING POTATOES

 The perfect roasted potato has a crisp, crunchy surface and a soft, fluffy interior. Varieties such as russet or long white are best for roasting, though small salad ones, such as round red, are also used in some cuisines, notably modern Italian. For extra flavor, roast potatoes with onions, garlic cloves in their skins, fresh thyme, or fresh rosemary. If potatoes are roasted alongside meat, the result will be less crisp, but they will have an excellent flavor.

Preparation

Potatoes can be roasted with or without the skins, but if peeled and cut into chunks, the pieces should be evenly sized so they cook at the same rate. Parboiling the potatoes first gives a soft interior and crisp edge. After parboiling, return the potatoes to the pan and swirl them to roughen the edges.

Oils and fats

The oil or fat used to roast potatoes is a matter of personal taste and regional tradition. Olive, safflower, or peanut oils are now the most common choices, largely for health reasons. However duck and goose fat famously give the most wonderful flavor. Lard and drippings, now rarely used, also give a good flavor.

Roasting method, times, and temperatures

Put oil or fat in a roasting pan large enough to hold the potatoes in a single layer, then heat in a preheated oven at 425°F. Add the potatoes to the hot oil (take care in case it sputters). Season with salt and pepper, then turn to coat with oil. Cook in the oven for 1 hour, turning occasionally, until crisp outside and tender inside. The time depends on the size of the potatoes.

FRIES

Potato varieties such as russet or long white, are the best choice for fries. Use a deep-fryer or large, deep saucepan, and never use oil at a depth of more than a third to half full. A wok, one-third full of oil, is a good alternative. Always reheat oil to the required temperature between batches, and lower the potatoes gently into the oil to prevent splashing. A frying basket, wire scoop, or slotted spoon let you turn and lift the potatoes easily. Do not overcrowd the pan, or the heat of the oil will be reduced and the potatoes will boil rather than fry, absorb too much oil, and become greasy and soggy rather than light and crispy.

Oils and fats

Peanut and corn oils cook at a high heat without burning, so are a good choice for deep-frying. Olive oil is wonderful but extravagant. Canola, safflower oil, and lard are also used. Always use clean oil, strain after use, and when reusing, remember what was cooked in it previously.

Frying method, times, and temperatures

Perfect fries are twice-cooked. Cut the potatoes into long strips ¼–½ inch thick, rinse well in cold water to remove the starch, then dry well. Fry in hot oil at 320°F for 5 minutes, or until tender but pale, then drain well. Increase the heat to 375°F and cook again for 1–2 minutes, or until crisp and golden. Check temperatures with a deep-frying thermometer or test-fry a cube of bread: it will turn golden in 1 minute at 320°F or in 40 seconds at 375°F.

Safety first!

Always dry the potato well after rinsing, as excess water makes the oil sputter and boil. Never leave the pan unattended, and clean up any spills immediately. Turn the handle of the pan away from the edge of the stove so it can't be knocked. If the oil starts to smoke, turn off the heat immediately. In the event of a fire, turn off the heat and cover the pan with a lid, baking sheet, or a thick, damp cloth. Do not attempt to move the pan or use water to extinguish the fire. Let the pan cool completely before moving it.

soups, salads and snacks

potage parmentier

WITH PARSLEY OIL AND CROUTONS

4 tablespoons unsalted butter

1 lb. potatoes, such as russet or long white, very thinly sliced

1 onion, thinly sliced

1 bay leaf

4 cups milk

sea salt and freshly ground black pepper

PARSLEY OIL

a large bunch fresh flat-leaf parsley

½ cup extra virgin olive oil

CROUTONS

3 tablespoons olive oil or 2 tablespoons unsalted butter

4 slices prosciutto or bacon

2 slices bread, crusts removed, cut or broken into ½-inch pieces

SERVES 4

To make the parsley oil, bring a saucepan of water to a boil, add the parsley, and blanch for 5–10 seconds. Drain and refresh in plenty of cold water. Drain well, then squeeze dry in a clean cloth. Chop the parsley and put in a blender. Add the olive oil and purée until very smooth. Either use as is, or strain first through a fine sieve, then again through 2 layers of cheesecloth or a paper coffee filter. Pour into a bottle and use within 1 week.

To make the soup (potage), melt the butter in a large, heavy saucepan, add the sliced potatoes and onion, stir, and cover. Cook without coloring for 5–8 minutes, stirring occasionally, until the onion is softened and translucent.

Add the bay leaf, milk, salt, and pepper, and bring to a boil. Reduce the heat, cover, and simmer for 15 minutes. Remove from the heat, discard the bay leaf, pour into a blender, and purée until smooth. Strain through a very fine sieve into a clean pan.

To make the croutons, heat the oil or melt the butter in a large skillet over moderate heat. Add the prosciutto or bacon and sauté for 5–6 minutes until crisp. Remove with a slotted spoon and drain on paper towels. Add the bread to the pan and sauté, turning frequently, until crisp and golden. Drain on paper towels.

Reheat the soup, season with salt and pepper, and serve sprinkled with the parsley oil. Crumble the prosciutto or bacon over the top, then add the croutons, or serve them both separately.

potato mussel soup

WITH ITALIAN SUN-DRIED TOMATOES

a pinch of saffron threads

½ cup boiling water

¾ cup dry white wine

2 lb. mussels, scrubbed, debearded, broken or open ones discarded

about 4 cups fish or chicken stock (see method)

2 tablespoons olive oil

1 onion, sliced

1–2 garlic cloves, crushed

1-inch piece fresh ginger, peeled and finely grated

1 lb. potatoes, cut into 1-inch cubes

1 large tomato, peeled and chopped

8–10 sun-dried tomatoes, finely chopped

grated zest and juice of 1 unwaxed orange

a sprig of thyme

sea salt and freshly ground black pepper

chopped fresh flat-leaf parsley, to serve

SERVES 4

Put the saffron in a small heatproof bowl, pour in the boiling water, and set aside to infuse. Pour the white wine into a pot large enough to hold all the mussels. Bring to a boil, add the mussels, cover with a tight-fitting lid, and cook, shaking the pan frequently, for 2–3 minutes, or until the mussels have opened.

Tip the mussels into a colander set over a bowl to collect the juice. Discard any mussels that have not opened. Remove two-thirds of the mussels from their shells, discard the empty shells, and set all the mussels aside. Strain the mussel liquid through a cheesecloth-lined sieve or paper coffee filter into a measuring cup. Measure the liquid and add fish or chicken stock or water to make 4 cups. Set aside.

Heat the olive oil in a large saucepan, add the onion, garlic, and ginger, and cook over medium heat for 5–10 minutes until the onion is softened and translucent. Add the potatoes, tomatoes, sun-dried tomatoes, and orange zest and cook for 1–2 minutes more. Add the reserved stock, the thyme, and the saffron in its soaking liquid, and bring to a boil. Reduce the heat and simmer for about 15 minutes until the potatoes are tender.

Add the orange juice and all the mussels. Reheat and season with salt and pepper. Serve sprinkled with the chopped parsley.

Many Australians with European roots still follow the cooking traditions of their country of origin. This Australian dish is a fine example of how the ingredients of one culture are absorbed into another.

Though creamy mayonnaise-style sauces are the traditional dressings for cold potato salads, highly flavored dressings based on extra virgin olive oil have become popular with chefs in America.

roasted warm potato salad

2 lb. small new or salad potatoes, unpeeled and scrubbed

½ cup extra virgin olive oil

1 small red onion, finely chopped

8 black olives, pitted and finely chopped

1½ tablespoons capers, rinsed and drained

6 sun-dried tomatoes in oil, drained and chopped

5 tablespoons chopped fresh flat-leaf parsley

1 tablespoon balsamic vinegar

sea salt and freshly ground black pepper

SERVES 4–6

Put the potatoes in a roasting pan, add 2 tablespoons of the olive oil, sprinkle with sea salt, and toss well to coat. Bake in a preheated oven at 400°F for 25–30 minutes, or until tender, turning the potatoes from time to time.

Meanwhile, put all the remaining ingredients in a large bowl, mix well, and season with salt and pepper.

Remove the potatoes from the oven, crush each potato slightly with a fork, and cut in half. Toss the still-warm potatoes in the bowl of dressing, mix well, and serve either warm or cold.

This Saudi Arabian salad combines a traditional Middle Eastern ingredient, the chickpea, with the more recent arrival, the potato. Both are particularly good for absorbing spicy flavors.

sultan's salad

¾ cup dried chickpeas (garbanzos)

1–2 garlic cloves, chopped

½ cup walnut halves, chopped

¼ cup chopped fresh flat-leaf parsley

2 tablespoons chopped fresh mint

¼ cup tahini paste

¼ cup freshly squeezed lemon juice

⅓ cup extra virgin olive oil

about ⅓ cup water

a pinch of paprika

1½ lb. new or salad potatoes, unpeeled and scrubbed

sea salt

TO SERVE (OPTIONAL)

2 tablespoons chopped walnuts

1 tablespoon toasted sesame seeds

4 sprigs of mint

SERVES 4

Put the chickpeas in a large bowl, cover with cold water, and let soak overnight.

The next day, drain the chickpeas and rinse well. Put them in a saucepan of unsalted cold water, bring to a boil, reduce the heat, and simmer for 50 minutes to 1 hour, or until tender. Drain well and reserve in a large bowl.

Put the garlic, walnuts, and herbs in the bowl of a food processor or blender. Blend until finely chopped. Add the tahini paste and 4 tablespoons lemon juice and blend well. With the motor running, add the olive oil in a thin steady stream until amalgamated. Add enough water to make a thin dressing. Pour the dressing into a bowl and season to taste with salt, paprika, and some more lemon juice if needed.

Bring a saucepan of lightly salted water to a boil, add the potatoes, and simmer for 15–20 minutes, or until tender. Drain well, then cut the potatoes in half and add to the chickpeas.

Pour the dressing over and toss the mixture well while still warm. Serve warm or cold, sprinkled with the chopped walnuts, toasted sesame seeds, and fresh mint sprigs, if using.

empanaditas

To make the spicy potato filling, bring a saucepan of lightly salted water to a boil, add the potatoes, and parboil for 2–3 minutes, drain well, and let cool. Put the remaining filling ingredients in a bowl and mix. Stir in the cooled potatoes, and season with salt and pepper.

Sift the flour and salt into a large bowl, stir in the butter, and add enough water to form a soft but firm dough. Knead briefly, wrap in plastic, and let rest for 30 minutes at room temperature.

Roll out the dough on a lightly floured surface to about ⅛ inch thick. Using the saucer as a template, cut out 16 circles, 5 inches in diameter. Knead and reroll any trimmings. Put 1 tablespoon filling on each round, a little off-center.

Dampen the edges of the dough with a little water and fold in half over the filling. Using the tines of a fork, press the edges together to seal them. Put the empanaditas on a tray and refrigerate for 30 minutes to 1 hour.

Fill a deep pan one-third full of oil. Heat to 375°F or until a cube of bread browns in 40 seconds. Fry the empanaditas in batches, turning once, for 3–5 minutes, or until golden brown. Drain on paper towels, then serve with a spicy fruit salsa, if using.

1⅔ cups all-purpose flour

½ teaspoon sea salt

7 tablespoons butter, melted

2–2½ tablespoons water

safflower oil, for deep-frying

spicy fruit salsa, to serve (optional)

SPICY POTATO FILLING

2 potatoes, cut into ¼-inch cubes

3 scallions, chopped

¾ cup frozen corn, defrosted

1–2 green chiles, seeded and finely chopped (optional)

3 oz. ricotta or goat cheese, crumbled, ½ cup

1 tablespoon chopped fresh marjoram

½ teaspoon paprika

sea salt and freshly ground black pepper

a saucer, 5 inches diameter

MAKES **16**

Empanaditas are small turnovers that are popular in Spain and Latin America. They usually have savory fillings, but can sometimes have a fruit filling and be served as a dessert.

India has dozens of different kinds of bread—plain, with spicy fillings, or flavored with spices, as here. They are usually served with curry or *dhaal*, but these roti are made smaller to be eaten as a snack.

mini potato roti

WITH COCONUT AND MINT CHUTNEY

1½ lb. large potatoes, such as russet or long white

2 fresh green chiles, seeded and finely chopped

½ teaspoon hot red pepper flakes

1 small onion, finely chopped

1 teaspoon sea salt

1 teaspoon ground cumin

1 teaspoon ground turmeric

2 tablespoons chopped fresh cilantro

2 tablespoons unsalted butter, melted

1 cup all-purpose flour

safflower oil, for frying

COCONUT AND MINT CHUTNEY

1½ cups grated fresh coconut or ⅔ cup unsweetened dried coconut

1 cup plain yogurt

1 fresh green chile, seeded and chopped

2 tablespoons chopped fresh mint

½ teaspoon sea salt

½ teaspoon sugar

MAKES **64**

To make the chutney, if using dried coconut put it in a bowl and cover with warm water. Let soak for 20 minutes, then strain through a sieve, pressing the coconut against the sides of the sieve to squeeze out any excess moisture. Put the coconut, yogurt, green chile, mint, salt, and sugar in a bowl. Mix well and set aside.

Put the potatoes in a large saucepan of lightly salted water and bring to a boil. Simmer for 20–30 minutes, or until tender. Drain and mash well. Add all the remaining ingredients, except the flour and oil, to the potatoes and mix well. Gradually mix in the flour until you have a soft dough. Divide the dough into 64 equal pieces. Taking one piece at a time, roll out on a floured board to a 3-inch circle. Continue with the remaining pieces of dough.

Heat a little oil in a heavy skillet and cook the roti 2 or 3 at a time for 1–2 minutes on each side, or until lightly browned. Serve with the coconut and mint chutney.

pizza con le patate

PIZZA DOUGH

0.6 oz. cake compressed fresh yeast,
or ¼ oz. sachet active dry yeast

a pinch of sugar

¾ cup warm water

2½ cups all-purpose flour,
plus extra for sprinkling

2 tablespoons olive oil

½ teaspoon sea salt

HERBED POTATO TOPPING

1 lb. potatoes, such as round red,
thinly sliced

2 tablespoons extra virgin olive oil

4 garlic cloves, crushed

leaves from 2 sprigs of rosemary

1 teaspoon sea salt flakes

2 baking trays

MAKES 2 PIZZAS, 10 INCHES DIAMETER

To make the pizza dough, put the fresh yeast, if using, and sugar in a small bowl and blend well. Mix in the warm water and leave for 10 minutes or until frothy. For other yeasts, follow the instructions on the package.

Sift the flour into a large bowl and make a well in the center. Pour in the yeast mixture, olive oil, and salt. Mix to form a soft but firm dough. Tip out onto a lightly floured surface and knead the dough for 10 minutes until smooth.

Divide the dough in half and form into 2 balls. Put the dough balls on a lightly floured surface or tray in a warm place and sprinkle them liberally with flour. (This will become the base of each pizza, the flour will make it easier to slide onto the baking tray.) Let rise for about 1 hour, or until doubled in size.

Put the baking trays in a preheated oven at 425°F until hot. Put the potato slices, olive oil, garlic, rosemary, and salt in a large bowl and stir to coat the potato.

Brush off any excess flour from the top of the dough, then transfer the balls to a work surface, and roll and pull each one into a large circle, about 10 inches in diameter. Spread the potato mixture evenly over both pizzas. Remove the trays from the oven and slide 1 pizza onto each one. Sprinkle with more olive oil and salt if using, then bake for 15–20 minutes, or until the potatoes are tender and the pizza bases lightly golden and crisp.

This is the Italian takeaway snack, *pizza al trancio*, usually found in bakeries where slices are heated up for you (*trancio* means "slice").

I discovered this delicious tart in New Mexico. The chile kick is quite subtle—roasting them softens their flavor. Potatoes are great partners for the verve of chile, and you can also add chile to the dough for more zest.

chile potato tart

WITH ROASTED TOMATOES AND GARLIC

3 tablespoons extra virgin olive oil

1½ lb. ripe red plum tomatoes,
halved lengthwise and seeded

4 whole garlic cloves, unpeeled

1 large red chile

1½ teaspoons sea salt flakes

1 tablespoon sugar

1 lb. potatoes, such as round red,
boiled in their skins for 15 minutes,
then peeled and thinly sliced

1¼ cups heavy cream, lightly
whipped and seasoned with salt
and pepper

sea salt and freshly ground
black pepper

DOUGH

1⅓ cups all-purpose flour

a pinch of sea salt

7 tablespoons unsalted butter,
cut into cubes

¼ cup freshly grated Parmesan cheese

1 red chile, seeded and very finely
chopped (optional)

a baking tray

*a tart pan, 10 inches diameter,
greased*

foil and baking beans

SERVES 6

To roast the tomatoes, lightly brush a baking tray with some of the olive oil and add the tomatoes, cut side up. Add the garlic and whole chile and sprinkle evenly with the remaining olive oil, salt, and sugar. Cook in a preheated oven at 350°F.

Remove the garlic from the oven after 10–15 minutes, or when soft, and squeeze the flesh into a bowl. Remove the chile after 15–20 minutes, or when the skin is blistered and slightly charred. Leave the tomatoes for 45–50 minutes total, or until very soft and slightly charred. Let the chile cool a little, then peel, seed, and finely chop. Add to the garlic. Scoop the tomato flesh out of the skins, add to the garlic, then mash with a fork. Season with salt and pepper.

To make the dough, sift the flour and salt into a bowl. Rub in the butter using your fingertips until the mixture resembles bread crumbs. Stir in the Parmesan and chile, if using. Add enough cold water to make a firm dough, then roll out on a lightly floured surface and use to line the greased tart pan. Lightly prick the base all over with a fork. Chill for 30 minutes. Heat a baking tray on the middle shelf of a preheated oven at 400°F. Line the tart crust with foil and baking beans. Put the tart crust on the tray, bake for 10–15 minutes, then remove the foil and beans.

Increase the oven temperature to 450°F. Spread the tomato mixture evenly over the tart base, then cover with concentric circles of potato slices. Pour the heavy cream over the potato and bake for 8–10 minutes, or until the top is lightly golden.

meat and poultry

straw potato pancakes

WITH GRILLED DUCK BREASTS

Scoop out the pomegranate seeds, discarding the white pith. Reserve 3 tablespoons of the seeds, cover, and chill.

To make the marinade, put the remaining seeds in a blender and process briefly. Strain through a fine sieve into a flat ceramic dish. Add the lemon zest, garlic, and ginger and stir. Add the duck to the marinade, turn to coat, cover, and chill for 12–24 hours, turning occasionally.

3 pomegranates, halved

zest of 1 preserved lemon, chopped

1 garlic clove, crushed

1-inch piece of fresh ginger, peeled and finely grated

4 small duck breasts, skin scored 3–4 times

1 lb. potatoes, such as round red

2 tablespoons clarified butter, plus extra if needed (see page 56)

1 tablespoon hazelnut oil

2 tablespoons honey

⅓ cup roasted hazelnuts, chopped

a few salad leaves

sea salt and freshly ground black pepper

SERVES 4

Cut the potatoes into thin julienne strips using a mandoline or sharp knife, and rinse in cold water. Drain, then rinse the potatoes 2–3 times to remove the starch. Drain, then dry well on a clean cloth. Put in a bowl and season with salt and pepper.

Heat the butter and oil in a large skillet. Add spoonfuls of the potato to make 4 cakes. Press down slightly and cook for 8–10 minutes. Turn over and cook for 5–6 minutes more. Remove the cakes and keep them warm.

Remove the duck from the marinade, reserving the marinade. Pat the duck dry and put on a preheated stove-top grill pan or outdoor grill. Cook, skin side down, for 5 minutes, then turn and cook 5 minutes longer until tender but still pink. Let rest for 5 minutes, then slice thinly.

Put the marinade and honey in a small saucepan, bring to a boil, and reduce until thickened. Season to taste with salt and pepper. To serve, put the pancakes on 4 warm plates, and top with the duck slices and reserved pomegranate seeds. Pour the reduced marinade over the top and sprinkle with chopped hazelnuts and salad leaves.

This is a wonderful yellow-orange stew, heavily scented with the spices of the Middle East.

chicken potato stew

WITH SEVILLE ORANGES

a large pinch of saffron threads

2 tablespoons olive oil

1 whole chicken, about 4 lb.,
cut into 8 pieces

2 tablespoons all-purpose flour

1 teaspoon sea salt, plus extra
to taste

crushed black seeds from
6 green cardamom pods

1 teaspoon whole cloves

1 teaspoon allspice berries

1 teaspoon whole black peppercorns

1 teaspoon whole pink peppercorns

2 cinnamon sticks, 3 inches each

freshly squeezed juice of 2 oranges

freshly squeezed juice of 2 lemons

1½ lb. potatoes, such as russet or
long white, cut into 3-inch chunks

1 unwaxed lemon, sliced

1 unwaxed orange, sliced

1–2 tablespoons rosewater (optional)

steamed rice, to serve (optional)

SERVES 4

Put the saffron threads in a small heatproof bowl and add boiling water to cover. Set aside to infuse.

Heat the olive oil in a large flameproof casserole dish and sauté the chicken to seal it, 2 or 3 pieces at a time, until lightly golden all over. Remove the pieces to a plate. Drain off all but 1 tablespoon of the fat from the dish. Add the flour and cook for 1–2 minutes, then add the saffron and its infusing water. Stir well.

Return the chicken pieces to the pot, add the salt, spices, and orange and lemon juices. Pour over enough water to cover (about 5 cups), and bring to a boil.

Add the potato pieces and the orange and lemon slices. Reduce the heat to low, cover with a lid, and simmer gently for 30–35 minutes, or until the potatoes are tender, occasionally skimming off any fat that rises to the surface.

Taste and season with salt and pepper, then stir in rosewater, if using, to taste. Serve with steamed rice, if using.

When mixed with wheat flour, or even made into potato flour, potatoes give a wonderful texture to baked goods. Dough made with potato, for instance, is light and crumbly.

2 lb. potatoes, such as russet or
long white

4 tablespoons unsalted butter

1 large egg, beaten

1 cup self-rising flour

1 teaspoon caraway seeds

sea salt and freshly ground
black pepper

CHICKEN LIVER FILLING

4 tablespoons unsalted butter

1 onion, finely chopped

1 celery stalk, finely chopped

1 carrot, finely chopped

1 lb. chicken livers, trimmed

½ teaspoon paprika

1 tablespoon tomato paste

½ cup white wine or chicken stock

¼ cup chopped fresh parsley

sea salt and freshly ground
black pepper

TO COAT

1 egg, beaten

⅓ cup fine dry bread crumbs

a saucer, 5 inches diameter

a baking tray, greased

MAKES 16–18

potato turnovers

WITH CHICKEN LIVERS

Put the potatoes in a large saucepan of lightly salted water and
bring to a boil. Simmer for 20–30 minutes, or until tender. When cool
enough to handle, peel the potatoes and press through a potato
ricer or food mill, or push through a sieve into a large bowl. Add the
butter, egg, salt, and pepper, and beat well. Gradually knead in the
flour and caraway seeds until well mixed. Transfer to a lightly floured
surface and roll out to ¼ inch thick. Let cool.

To make the filling, melt the butter in a skillet. Add the onion, celery,
and carrot and cook for about 5 minutes, until softened and lightly
golden. Increase the heat, add the chicken livers, and cook for
5 minutes, stirring frequently, until sealed all over. Stir in the paprika,
tomato paste, wine or stock, and chopped parsley. Season with salt
and pepper and let cool.

Using the saucer as a template, cut the potato dough into circles
5 inches diameter. Put 1 tablespoon filling on each circle, a little
off-center. Fold the dough over the filling and press the edges firmly
together. Put on the greased baking tray, brush with the some
beaten egg, sprinkle with bread crumbs, and bake in a preheated
oven at 400°F for 20–30 minutes, or until golden. Serve as a snack
or as a light lunch with salad.

A very simple, delicious curry with all the flavors of Thailand. Fish sauce (*nam pla*), Thai curry pastes, and kaffir lime leaves are available in large supermarkets and Southeast Asian stores.

2 tablespoons safflower oil

1½ lb. boneless chicken (breasts or thighs), cut into large chunks

2–3 tablespoons red or green Thai curry paste

2¾ cups canned coconut milk

2½ tablespoons Thai fish sauce (*nam pla*)

2 tablespoons sugar

1 lb. new potatoes, unpeeled, scrubbed, and cut in half

½ teaspoon sea salt

1–2 tablespoons freshly squeezed lime juice

TO SERVE

⅓ cup unsalted roasted peanuts

3 scallions, cut into fine shreds and put in a bowl of cold water

Thai basil or cilantro, chopped

2 kaffir lime leaves, thinly sliced (optional)

steamed jasmine rice

SERVES 4

thai chicken curry

WITH POTATOES AND COCONUT MILK

Heat the oil in a large wok or skillet, add the chicken pieces, in batches if necessary, and sauté them briefly on all sides to seal. Remove the chicken pieces to a bowl.

Add the curry paste to the pan and stir-fry for about 30 seconds to release the aromas of the chiles and spices. Add the coconut milk, fish sauce, and sugar and stir well. Return the sautéed chicken pieces to the pan, together with any juices that have accumulated in the bowl.

Bring the mixture to a boil, then add the potato halves and salt. Reduce the heat, cover the pan, and simmer for 15–20 minutes, or until the chicken is cooked and the potatoes are tender.

Stir in the lime juice to taste and more salt, if needed. Serve sprinkled with the peanuts, drained scallion strips, basil or cilantro, and the kaffir lime leaf strips, if using. Steamed jasmine rice is an authentic accompaniment.

potato-crusted lamb

WITH POACHED TAMARILLOS

1½ lb. potatoes, such as round red

1 garlic clove, crushed

2 tablespoons chopped fresh chives

2 tablespoons chopped fresh
flat-leaf parsley

1 tablespoon fresh thyme leaves

2 large egg yolks, beaten

12 lamb rib chops, very well trimmed,
with all fat removed and the bone
scraped clean

3 tablespoons olive oil

sea salt and freshly ground
black pepper

sprigs of thyme, to serve

POACHED TAMARILLOS

6 tamarillos

⅔ cup port or red wine

⅔ cup chicken stock

3 tablespoons honey

2 inches cinnamon stick

½ teaspoon crushed coriander seeds

a strip of unwaxed orange zest

SERVES 4

Grate the potatoes finely and do not rinse. Wrap in a clean cloth and squeeze to extract any excess liquid. Put the grated potato in a bowl and add the garlic, herbs, and egg yolks. Season with salt and pepper, then mix well. Divide into 12 parts and wrap each lamb chop completely with a portion of the mixture.

To prepare the tamarillos, use a sharp knife to cut a small cross at the pointed end of each one. Bring a saucepan of water to a boil, add the tamarillos, and blanch for 30 seconds. Lift out with a slotted spoon and plunge them into cold water.

To make the sauce, carefully peel all the tamarillos, and finely chop 2 of them. Put the chopped tamarillos in a shallow pan, then add the port or red wine, stock, honey, cinnamon, crushed coriander seeds, and orange zest. Bring to a boil, reduce the heat, add the whole tamarillos, and simmer for 3–4 minutes. Lift the whole fruit out of the sauce and set aside. Increase the heat and boil the sauce rapidly for 2–3 minutes or until well reduced.

Heat the oil over moderate heat in 2 large heavy-bottom skillets. Add the lamb chops and cook for 3–4 minutes on each side, or until the potato is cooked and crispy and the lamb is still pink. Slice the tamarillos, but leave them attached at the stalk, then return them to the sauce and reheat gently.

To serve, put 3 chops and 1 sliced tamarillo on each plate. Spoon a little sauce over and sprinkle with thyme sprigs.

Tamarillos are a sub-tropical fruit.
They can be bought in large
supermarkets, but if unavailable,
substitute plums or apricots.

These little fried cakes of potato and chorizo with a crisp corn salsa are based on a dish I discovered in Mexico.

1½ lb. potatoes, unpeeled and
well scrubbed

3 chorizo sausages, 3 oz. each,
peeled and crumbled

1 garlic clove, crushed

4 scallions, chopped

8 oz. fresh goat cheese,
2 cups, crumbled

1 large egg, beaten

½ cup fine dry bread crumbs

olive oil, for frying

salad leaves, to serve

sea salt and freshly ground
black pepper

CORN SALSA VERDE

1 tablespoon Dijon mustard

1 tablespoon freshly squeezed
lime juice, or wine vinegar

⅔ cup extra-virgin olive oil

2 tablespoons capers, rinsed, drained,
and chopped

½ cup frozen corn, defrosted

2 scallions, finely chopped

1–2 garlic cloves, finely chopped

6 tablespoons chopped fresh
flat-leaf parsley

6 tablespoons chopped fresh cilantro

1–2 green chiles, finely chopped

sea salt and freshly ground
black pepper

SERVES 6

tortitas de papa

WITH CHORIZO AND CORN SALSA VERDE

Put the potatoes in a large saucepan of lightly salted water and bring to
a boil. Simmer for 20–30 minutes, or until tender. Drain well and, when
cool enough to handle, peel and pass through a potato ricer or food mill,
or push through a sieve into a large bowl.

Heat a nonstick skillet, add the chorizo, and sauté gently for about
10 minutes, or until the fat renders. Remove the chorizo with a slotted
spoon, let cool slightly, then add to the potato. Add the garlic, scallions,
and goat cheese and mix. Add the egg, salt, and pepper and mix well.

Divide the mixture into 18 parts and form into small flat cakes. Roll each
one in the bread crumbs, pressing gently so the crumbs stick. Set aside
while you make the salsa.

To make the salsa verde, put the mustard in a small bowl and beat in the
lime juice or wine vinegar. Continue beating, adding the olive oil in a thin
stream until amalgamated. Stir in the remaining ingredients, then season
with salt and pepper to taste.

Heat the oil in a large nonstick skillet and sauté the potato cakes in
batches until golden brown all over (8–10 minutes). Drain on paper
towels. Keep them warm while you cook the remaining cakes.

Serve with the salsa verde and crisp salad leaves, such as the mizuna,
arugula, and baby spinach shown here.

one-dish meals

This combination of pasta and potatoes comes from an Italian-Australian friend of mine. Though not traditionally Italian, it is characteristic of the "fusion food" found in Australia.

pasta and potatoes

WITH MACADAMIA PESTO

1 lb. new or salad potatoes, unpeeled and scrubbed

1 lb. tagliatelle

MACADAMIA PESTO

a large bunch fresh basil leaves

½ cup unsalted macadamias, chopped

2 garlic cloves, chopped

¾ cup extra virgin olive oil

1 cup freshly grated Parmesan cheese, plus extra to serve (optional)

sea salt and freshly ground black pepper

serves 4

To make the pesto, put the basil, macadamias, and garlic in a blender or food processor and process until finely chopped. With the motor running, gradually add the oil in a thin stream until amalgamated. Scrape into a bowl, stir in the Parmesan, and season to taste with salt and pepper.

Bring a saucepan of lightly salted water to a boil, add the potatoes, and cook for 10–15 minutes, or until just tender. Drain and let cool slightly, then peel and cut into ¼-inch slices.

Cook the pasta in a large saucepan of lightly salted boiling water, according to the package instructions. Drain in a colander, but leave 2–3 tablespoons of the cooking water in the bottom of the pan. (A small amount of cooking water will bind the sauce and help it cling to the pasta.)

Return the pasta to the pan, add the potato slices and half of the pesto, and mix well. (Refrigerate the remaining pesto to use in another dish.) Taste and season with salt and pepper. Serve immediately, sprinkled with extra Parmesan, if using.

This recipe is based on a Persian dish but with fava beans added. Use frozen fava beans or regular peas if you can't find fresh favas.

persian potato omelet

1½ cups shelled fava beans or regular peas, defrosted if frozen

1 lb. cooked potatoes, mashed

6 large eggs, beaten

1 teaspoon ground turmeric

6 scallions, chopped

2 tablespoons chopped fresh cilantro

1 tablespoon chopped fresh flat-leaf parsley

2 tablespoons unsalted butter

sea salt and freshly ground black pepper

SERVES 6–8

If using young fresh fava beans, blanch them in lightly salted boiling water for 5–6 minutes (longer for older ones), then drain. Refresh in cold water, then drain again. Pop the fresh or defrosted frozen fava beans out of their skins, set aside, discarding the skins.

Put the mashed potato in a large bowl, then stir in the beaten eggs and ground turmeric. Fold in the fava beans, scallions, and herbs, and season with salt and pepper.

Put the butter in a heavy nonstick skillet with a heatproof handle and melt over moderate heat. Add the potato mixture. Reduce the heat to very low and cook without stirring for 15–20 minutes, or until the eggs have set and the base is golden brown (check by lifting the edge of the omelet with a spatula).

Put the pan under a preheated broiler to brown the top of the omelet, then slide it onto a large plate or tray and cut into small squares or wedges. Serve hot or cold.

The success of gnocchi depends on lightly mixing the potato and flour to the right consistency—smooth and slightly sticky. If you overmix, the gnocchi will be heavy.

potato gnocchi

WITH WALNUT AND ARUGULA PESTO

To make the pesto, put the arugula, walnuts, and garlic in a blender or food processor and blend until finely chopped. Add the olive oil and blend well to form a purée. Scrape the mixture into a bowl and stir in the Parmesan. Taste and adjust the seasoning with salt and pepper. Set aside to develop the flavors while you make the gnocchi.

Put the potatoes in a saucepan with cold salted water to cover. Bring to a boil and cook for 20–30 minutes, or until soft. Drain well, let cool slightly, then peel. While still warm, press through a potato ricer or food mill, or push through a sieve into a large bowl. Beat the flour into the potatoes, a little at a time. Stop adding flour when the mixture is smooth and slightly sticky. Season with salt to taste.

Transfer the mixture to a well-floured board, then roll out the dough into long sausages about ½ inch in diameter. Cut each sausage into short pieces about 1 inch long. Put each piece on the end of your thumb and press the prongs of a fork lightly over the top. The pieces will be hollow on one side and grooved on the other. Put them on a floured plate as you make them.

Bring a large saucepan of water to a boil. Add 20–25 pieces of gnocchi to the pan at a time. They will quickly rise to the surface. Cook for 10–15 seconds more, then remove with a slotted spoon and put in a bowl while you cook the rest. Add the pesto to the bowl and gently turn the gnocchi in the mixture until they are well covered. Serve immediately, sprinkled with extra Parmesan.

1½ lb. large potatoes, such as russet or long white, cut into even pieces

¾ cup all-purpose flour, plus extra for rolling

sea salt, to taste

WALNUT AND ARUGULA PESTO

a large bunch arugula leaves, roughly chopped

¼ cup chopped walnuts

2 garlic cloves

½ cup extra virgin olive oil

¼ cup freshly grated Parmesan cheese, plus extra to serve

sea salt and freshly ground black pepper

SERVES 4

Dhaal baht (rice and lentils) is a staple meal for millions of Indians and Nepalis. In this recipe, *aloo* (potatoes) are added to that traditional duo; they are particularly desirable for their ability to absorb the wonderful flavors of Indian spices.

1¼ cups yellow lentils, toor dhaal

3 tablespoons safflower oil

½ teaspoon mustard seeds

½ teaspoon fenugreek seeds

1 teaspoon grated fresh ginger

1 teaspoon crushed garlic

1 teaspoon chili powder

1½ teaspoons ground coriander

½ teaspoon ground turmeric

4 tomatoes, peeled and chopped

2½ cups water

1 teaspoon sea salt

1½ lb. potatoes, such as russet or long white, cut into ¾-inch chunks

sea salt and freshly ground black pepper

TO SERVE

2 tablespoons chopped fresh cilantro, plus extra sprigs

½ teaspoon garam masala*

basmati rice

SERVES 4

indian potato curry

WITH TOOR DHAAL (YELLOW LENTILS)

Wash the lentils well in several changes of water. Heat the oil in a large saucepan over low heat. Add the mustard and fenugreek seeds. When they begin to pop, stir in the ginger and garlic and fry for 30 seconds.

Add the chili powder and ground coriander and turmeric and stir-fry for a further 30 seconds. Add the tomatoes, lentils, water, and salt, then bring to a boil. Reduce the heat, cover and simmer for 20–30 minutes, or until the lentils are just soft.

Add the potatoes and simmer over low heat for 10–15 minutes, or until the potatoes are tender. Season with salt and pepper.

Serve sprinkled with chopped cilantro, garam masala, and sprigs of fresh cilantro. Basmati rice makes a suitable accompaniment.

*Note: Garam masala is a spice blend which originates from northern India—*garam* means "hot", *masala* means "spice." It is available from Asian stores and larger supermarkets. If you want to make your own, put the following in a spice grinder: 2 tablespoons cumin seeds, 2 teaspoons black cumin seeds, seeds from 2 green cardamom pods, 2-inch piece of cinnamon stick, 5 whole cloves, and 2 bay leaves. Grind all the spices to a fine powder. Store in an airtight container.

potato gratin

WITH HERBS, SPINACH, AND CHEESE

1 garlic clove, crushed

1 tablespoon unsalted butter, melted

1 lb. trimmed fresh spinach,
about 4 cups

3 large eggs, beaten

2¼ cups heavy cream

1¼ cups grated Gruyère cheese

1½ cups chopped fresh herbs, such as
chives, parsley, chervil, or sorrel

a pinch of freshly grated nutmeg

a pinch of cayenne pepper

2½ lb. large waxy potatoes,
thinly sliced

sea salt and freshly ground
black pepper

TO SERVE

salad greens

vinaigrette dressing, to taste

sea salt and cracked black pepper

a springform cake pan,
9 inches diameter

SERVES 6–8

Mix the garlic and melted butter in a bowl and use to grease the springform cake pan.

Wash the spinach and put in a large saucepan with just the water that is left clinging to the leaves. Cover and heat, stirring once, until the spinach has just wilted. Drain well and squeeze out any excess moisture. Chop finely.

Put the eggs and heavy cream in a bowl and beat well. Stir in the chopped cooked spinach, and two-thirds of the Gruyère. Add the herbs and season well with nutmeg, cayenne, salt, and pepper.

Cover the base of the cake pan with a layer of sliced potato and spread evenly with a spoonful of the cream and spinach mixture. Continue the layers, finishing with a layer of potato. Sprinkle with the remaining Gruyère, then cover the pan with foil.

Put the cake pan in a roasting pan and pour enough boiling water around the cake pan to come half way up the sides. Carefully put in a preheated oven and cook at 350°F for about 1½ hours, or until the potatoes are tender—test by piercing the center with a knife. Remove the foil for the last 15 minutes to let the top brown.

Unclip the pan and cut into wedges. Serve hot or cold seasoned with salt and lots of cracked black pepper, and with salad leaves sprinkled with vinaigrette dressing.

A wonderful creamy gratin of potatoes layered with spinach, herbs, Gruyère, and heavy cream. It can be served hot or cold and would make an easily transportable picnic dish.

This soufflé of hot, fluffy potato with nuggets of mozzarella and fontina cheese melting through is the perfect comfort food.

3 tablespoons unsalted butter, melted

½ cup dry bread crumbs

3 lb. floury potatoes, such as russet or long white, unpeeled

4 tablespoons unsalted butter, at room temperature

¾ cup milk, warmed

2 large eggs, plus 1 egg yolk, beaten

½ cup freshly grated Parmesan cheese

4 oz. mozzarella cheese, drained and cut into cubes

4 oz. fontina or Emmental cheese, cut into cubes

sea salt and freshly ground black pepper

arugula leaves, to serve

ALMOND-PARSLEY PESTO

1 bunch of fresh flat-leaf parsley, washed and stalks removed

⅓ cup almonds (with brown skins left on), toasted in the oven until golden, then cooled

1 cup extra virgin olive oil

¾ cup Parmesan cheese, grated

sea salt and freshly ground black pepper

a soufflé dish or cake pan, 9 inches diameter

SERVES 4

potato soufflé

WITH MOZZARELLA AND ALMOND-PARSLEY PESTO

To make the almond-parsley pesto, grind the parsley, toasted almonds, and 2 tablespoons olive oil to a fairly coarse texture using a mortar and pestle or a food processor. Scrape into a bowl, then stir in the remaining oil and Parmesan. Season with salt and pepper.

Generously grease the soufflé dish or cake pan with half the melted butter, then coat well with half the bread crumbs, shaking out any excess.

Put the potatoes in a large saucepan of lightly salted water and bring to a boil. Simmer for 20–30 minutes, or until tender. Drain well and when cool enough to handle, peel and press the warm potatoes through a potato ricer or food mill, or push through a sieve into a large bowl. Add the butter and warm milk and mix. Pour in the beaten eggs, add the Parmesan, and season with salt and pepper. Mix well.

Spoon half the potato mixture into the prepared soufflé dish or cake pan, pushing it up against the sides. Spread the cheese cubes over the top, then cover with the remaining potato mixture. Brush with the remaining 1½ tablespoons melted butter and sprinkle with the remaining ¼ cup bread crumbs.

Cook in a preheated oven at 350°F for 20 minutes, then increase the oven temperature to 425°F and cook for a further 10 minutes, or until the top is golden.

Sprinkle with the pesto and serve with some arugula leaves.

accompaniments

This method of cracking the potatoes and cooking them in wine comes from Cyprus. Cooked slowly with coriander seeds, the potatoes absorb all the wonderful juices.

cracked new potatoes

IN CORIANDER AND RED WINE

2 lb. small new potatoes, unpeeled, scrubbed, and dried

¼ cup olive oil

1 tablespoon coriander seeds, crushed

⅔ cup red wine

¼ cup chopped fresh cilantro

sea salt and freshly ground black pepper

SERVES 4–6

Put the potatoes in a clean cloth and, using a wooden mallet or other heavy kitchen implement, thump the potatoes to crack them open. (Don't be overzealous or you will end up with raw mashed potato!)

Heat the oil gently in a skillet large enough to hold the potatoes in a single layer. Add the potatoes, coriander seeds, salt, and pepper and cook, turning the potatoes occasionally, until lightly golden all over.

Add the wine, let it boil, then reduce the heat. Cover the pan and simmer gently, shaking the pan occasionally, for 15–20 minutes, or until the potatoes are tender.

Remove the pan from the heat and stir in the chopped cilantro. Serve as an accompaniment to meat or poultry.

champ

Put the potatoes in a large saucepan of lightly salted water and bring to a boil. Simmer for 20–30 minutes, or until tender. Drain well. Meanwhile, put the scallions in a saucepan with the milk, bring to a boil, then simmer for 2–3 minutes. Remove from the heat and let infuse for 10 minutes.

1½ lb. potatoes, such as russet or long white

10 scallions, including the green tops, chopped

1¼ cups milk

4 tablespoons butter, plus extra for serving

2 cups blue cheese, crumbled, 8 oz. (optional)

sea salt and freshly ground black pepper

SERVES 4

Press the potatoes through a potato ricer or food mill, or push through a sieve into a large bowl. Beat in the milk and scallion mixture, then the butter, salt, and pepper. Transfer to a clean pan and reheat gently. To serve, spoon into small bowls in mounds, make a hollow in the top, and insert more butter and blue cheese, if using.

VARIATIONS

COLCANNON (SHOWN ABOVE LEFT), IRELAND
Kale, cabbage, or another leafy green vegetable is used instead of the scallions and cheese. It is served in the same way as champ, or formed into cakes and sautéed in butter to form a crunchy crust.

CLAPSHOT, SCOTLAND
Follow the recipe for champ, but omit the scallions (although you can add these, if you prefer) and blue cheese. Add 1½ lb. boiled mashed rutabagas. Chopped chives or bacon fat may also be added.

KAILKENNY, SCOTTISH HIGHLANDS
Follow the recipe for colcannon, adding ½ cup cream.

RUMBLEDETHUMPS, SCOTTISH BORDERS
1½ lb. each of cooked potatoes and cabbage are thumped (mashed) then rumbled (mixed) with black pepper and 1 stick butter. It is then topped with cheese and broiled until brown.

Champ is pure comfort food. Dip each forkful of potato in the little pool of butter before eating. Blue cheese, especially Irish Cashel Blue, is my personal optional addition!

This is perhaps the best-known of all Swedish potato recipes. The original uses butter and bread crumbs, and sometimes Parmesan cheese is added.

bay-roasted hasselbacks

24 small potatoes, unpeeled and scrubbed

approximately 20 fresh bay leaves, torn in half lengthwise

1 tablespoon unsalted butter

3 tablespoons olive oil

1–2 garlic cloves, crushed

sea salt flakes and freshly ground black pepper

SERVES 4–6

To prepare the potatoes, put 2 chopsticks side by side on a board and put a potato lengthwise between them. Using a sharp knife, and holding the sticks and potato in place, make crosswise cuts ⅛ inch apart, cutting just down to the sticks. Alternatively, spear each potato lengthwise with a skewer about ¼ inch from the base, slice across the potato as far as the skewer, then remove the skewer.

Insert a couple of pieces of bay leaf, or a whole bay leaf if small, in each sliced potato. Melt the butter with the olive oil in a heavy-based roasting pan over moderate heat. Stir in the garlic, and carefully add the potatoes in a single layer—take care, the oil may sputter. Move them around for 2–3 minutes to color slightly, then season with sea salt flakes and pepper.

Place the pan in a preheated oven at 375°F and roast for 25–30 minutes, or until the potatoes are golden brown and tender. As they cook, the potatoes will open out like a fan.

Serve as an accompaniment to meat or poultry, or to baked or roasted fish.

This traditional French cooking method has been enthusiastically adopted by modern American chefs. Cooking in a package means that the flavor and goodness of the potatoes is retained as they cook in their own steam. Let your guests open the packages at the table.

potatoes en papillote

SCENTED WITH FRESH HERBS

1 lb. very small new potatoes, unpeeled and scrubbed

4 tablespoons unsalted butter

4 sprigs of fresh herbs such as thyme, tarragon, chervil, mint, or rosemary

1 large egg, beaten

sea salt

a baking tray

parchment paper

SERVES 4

Cut out 4 sheets of parchment paper, 12 x 15 inches each, and fold in half lengthwise. Draw a large curve from the folded side in the shape of half a heart. Cut along the line and open the paper.

Put one-quarter of the potatoes on one-half of each piece of paper. Dot the butter evenly over the potatoes, sprinkle with sea salt, and add an herb sprig to each one.

Brush the edges of the paper with the beaten egg and fold over. Starting from the rounded end, pleat the edges together in small folds so that each package is completely sealed. Twist the ends together.

Put the packages on a baking tray and cook in a preheated oven at 400°F for 25–30 minutes, or until the packages are well puffed and the potatoes are tender. Serve immediately.

swiss rösti

Put the whole potatoes in a large saucepan and cover with cold water. Bring to a boil and cook for 10–15 minutes, or until the potatoes are just tender. Drain well, let cool slightly, peel, then grate coarsely into a large bowl.

Heat 2 tablespoons of the clarified butter in a skillet, add the onion and bacon, and cook for 5–6 minutes, or until the onions are softened. Add this mixture to the bowl of potato, season with salt and pepper, and mix well.

2 lb. potatoes, unpeeled and scrubbed

¾ cup clarified butter*

1 onion, chopped

4 oz. prosciutto or bacon, cut into thin strips

1 lb. wild or portobello mushrooms, or a mixture of both, cut in halves or quarters if large

2 tablespoons chopped fresh flat-leaf parsley

sea salt and freshly ground black pepper

SERVES 4

Heat half the remaining butter in a skillet, add the potato mixture, and press down slightly with the back of a spoon to form a large pancake. Cook for 10 minutes, adding a little extra butter around the edges and shaking the skillet occasionally.

Cover the skillet with a plate and carefully invert so that the pancake falls onto the plate. Return the skillet to the heat, add more butter, then carefully slide the rösti back in to the skillet to cook the other side. Add more butter around the edges and cook until golden, about 7 minutes. Remove from the heat and keep it warm.

Heat the remaining butter in a skillet. Add the mushrooms and sauté, stirring occasionally, for 3–5 minutes, or until tender but still firm. Season with salt and pepper, then stir in the parsley.

Serve the rösti topped with the mushrooms. An alternative option is to divide the rösti mixture into 4 parts before cooking to serve as a small starter—or vary the topping according to taste, and serve with a few salad leaves, like arugula.

*Note: To clarify butter, melt over gentle heat, then let cool. Skim off the pure butter and discard the solids and water.

These Swiss pancakes can also be served topped with Gruyère cheese, fried eggs, or served separately with meat and sausages.

Two of the finest French potato dishes are *gratin dauphinois* and *pommes à la dauphinoise*. They are very similar to each other, but in the latter, sliced potatoes are baked with cream and garlic. To make *gratin dauphinois* a mixture of eggs, milk, and cream is poured over the potatoes, they are then topped with cheese before baking.

pommes à la dauphinoise

Bring a small saucepan of water to a boil. Add the garlic, reduce the heat, and simmer for 20 minutes, or until very tender. Remove the garlic, then crush well to a purée using a mortar and pestle, or press through a fine sieve.

4 garlic cloves

¾ cup milk

2 cups heavy cream

2 lb. potatoes, such as russet or long white, sliced into ¼-inch slices

sea salt and freshly ground white pepper

a roasting pan or baking dish, about 6 x 10 inches, or a round cake pan, 9 inches diameter, greased

SERVES 4

Put the puréed garlic in a saucepan with the milk and cream, season well with salt and pepper, bring to a boil, then remove from the heat.

Arrange the potato slices in the greased roasting pan, dish, or cake pan in 6 or 7 layers.

Pour the cream mixture over and press the potatoes down. The cream should come to just below the top potato layer. Cook in a preheated oven at 325°F for 1½–2 hours, pressing the potatoes down gently every 20 minutes.

The cream will be absorbed gradually and the potatoes will become compressed and more solid as they cook. If there appears to be too much liquid, remove some with a spoon. When the top is colored, stop pressing.

Test with a knife to be sure the potatoes are cooked. Remove from the oven and let rest in a warm place for 10 minutes. Spoon straight from the dish or cut out shapes with pastry cutters for a more elegant serving.

baking

golden potato biscuits

WITH PARMESAN AND PROSCIUTTO

4 slices of prosciutto or bacon, about 2 oz., cut into small pieces

1 cup all-purpose flour

2 teaspoons baking powder

½ teaspoon sea salt

4 tablespoons unsalted butter, cut into cubes, plus extra for serving

½ cup cooked mashed potato

2 oz. Parmesan cheese, cut into tiny cubes

1 teaspoon dried oregano

about 2 tablespoons milk

1 egg yolk, beaten, to glaze

a fluted cutter, 2½ inches diameter

a baking tray, well greased

MAKES 10

Heat a skillet without oil and dry-fry the prosciutto or bacon for 5–6 minutes, or until crispy. Remove with a slotted spoon and drain on paper towels.

Sift the flour, baking powder, and salt into a large bowl. Add the butter and rub in using your fingertips until the mixture resembles bread crumbs.

Add the potato, Parmesan, oregano, and cooked prosciutto or bacon pieces and mix well. Add enough milk to form a soft but firm dough. Turn out onto a lightly floured surface and knead briefly. Roll out the dough to ½ inch thick, then stamp out rounds using the fluted cutter. Reroll any trimmings and cut more rounds to make about 10 biscuits in total.

Put the biscuits on the prepared baking tray and brush the tops with the beaten egg. Cook in a preheated oven at 425°F for 10–15 minutes, or until golden brown and well risen. Transfer to a wire rack and let cool a little. Serve while still warm, spread with unsalted butter.

honey potato bread

WITH SAFFRON AND A POPPYSEED GLAZE

8 oz. potatoes, such as russet or
long white, cut into even pieces

a large pinch of saffron threads

2¾ cups bread flour

1 teaspoon sea salt

1½ teaspoons active dry yeast

2 tablespoons honey

6 tablespoons unsalted butter, melted

2 large egg yolks, beaten

¾ cup raisins

POPPYSEED GLAZE

1 large egg white, beaten

1 tablespoon black poppyseeds

2 baking trays, greased

MAKES 2 LOAVES

Put the potatoes in a large saucepan of lightly salted water and bring
to a boil. Simmer for 20–30 minutes, or until tender. Drain, reserving
1 cup of the cooking water in a bowl. Add the saffron threads to the
reserved water and let steep for about 30 minutes.

Press the drained potatoes through a potato ricer or food mill, or push
through a fine sieve into a large bowl. Add the reserved potato water and
saffron and mix well.

Sift the flour and salt into a large bowl and stir in the dry yeast. Add the
potato mixture, honey, butter, egg yolks, and raisins. Mix well to form
a soft but firm dough. Transfer the dough to a lightly floured surface and
knead for 10 minutes. Transfer to an oiled bowl, cover, and leave in
a warm place for 1–1½ hours or until doubled in size.

Transfer the dough to a floured surface, punch down, and knead for
a further 5 minutes. Cut in half and form into 2 round loaves. Put 1 loaf on
each greased baking tray and score each one with a knife in a criss-cross
pattern. Cover loosely and let rise again in a warm place for 45 minutes to
1 hour, until doubled in size once more.

Brush the tops of the loaves with egg white and sprinkle with poppyseeds.
Cook in a preheated oven at 400°F for 40 minutes or until the bottom of
the loaf sounds hollow when tapped. Let cool on a wire rack. Eat within
5 days or freeze for up to 1 month.

An updated version of an old-fashioned bread.
Potato and potato flour produce bread with a moist
texture that keeps well and is very good toasted.

index

conversion charts

Weights and measures have been
rounded up or down slightly to
make measuring easier.

Volume equivalents:

American	Metric	Imperial
1 teaspoon	5 ml	
1 tablespoon	15 ml	
¼ cup	60 ml	2 fl.oz.
⅓ cup	75 ml	2½ fl.oz.
½ cup	125 ml	4 fl.oz.
⅔ cup	150 ml	5 fl.oz. (¼ pint)
¾ cup	175 ml	6 fl.oz.
1 cup	250 ml	8 fl.oz.

Weight equivalents:

Imperial	Metric
1 oz.	25 g
2 oz.	50 g
3 oz.	75 g
4 oz.	125 g
5 oz.	150 g
6 oz.	175 g
7 oz.	200 g
8 oz. (½ lb.)	250 g
9 oz.	275 g
10 oz.	300 g
11 oz.	325 g
12 oz.	375 g
13 oz.	400 g
14 oz.	425 g
15 oz.	475 g
16 oz. (1 lb.)	500 g
2 1b.	1 kg

Measurements:

Inches	Cm
¼ inch	5 mm
½ inch	1 cm
¾ inch	1.5 cm
1 inch	2.5 cm
2 inches	5 cm
3 inches	7 cm
4 inches	10 cm
5 inches	12 cm
6 inches	15 cm
7 inches	18 cm
8 inches	20 cm
9 inches	23 cm
10 inches	25 cm
11 inches	28 cm
12 inches	30 cm

Oven temperatures:

110°C	(225°F)	Gas ¼
120°C	(250°F)	Gas ½
140°C	(275°F)	Gas 1
150°C	(300°F)	Gas 2
160°C	(325°F)	Gas 3
180°C	(350°F)	Gas 4
190°C	(375°F)	Gas 5
200°C	(400°F)	Gas 6
220°C	(425°F)	Gas 7
230°C	(450°F)	Gas 8
240°C	(475°F)	Gas 9